Ella and the Imp
and
Dad Has a Nap

PHASE 2 AND 3

2b

Level 2 – Red

Helpful Hints for Reading at Home

The graphemes (written letters) and phonemes (units of sound) used throughout this series are aligned with Letters and Sounds. This offers a consistent approach to learning whether reading at home or in the classroom. Books levelled as 'a' are an introduction to this band. Readers can advance to 'b' where graphemes are consolidated and further graphemes are introduced.

HERE IS A LIST OF NEW GRAPHEMES FOR THIS PHASE OF LEARNING. AN EXAMPLE OF THE PRONUNCIATION CAN BE FOUND IN BRACKETS.

Phase 3			
s (sat)	a (cat)	t (tap)	p (tap)
i (pin)	n (net)	m (man)	d (dog)
g (go)	o (sock)	c (cat)	k (kin)
ck (sack)	e (elf)	u (up)	r (rabbit)
h (hut)	b (ball)	f (fish)	ff (off)
l (lip)	ll (ball)	ss (hiss)	
ure (sure)	er (corner)		

Phase 3 Set 6			
j (jam)	v (van)	w (win)	x (mix)

HERE ARE SOME WORDS WHICH YOUR CHILD MAY FIND TRICKY.

Phase 2 Tricky Words			
the	to	I	no
go	into		

Phase 3 Tricky Words			
he	you	she	they
we	all	me	are
be	my	was	her

TOP TIPS FOR HELPING YOUR CHILD TO READ:

- Allow children time to break down unfamiliar words into units of sound and then encourage children to string these sounds together to create the word.

- Encourage your child to point out any focus phonics when they are used.

- Read through the book more than once to grow confidence.

- Ask simple questions about the text to assess understanding.

- Encourage children to use illustrations as prompts.

This book is a 'b' level and is a red level 2 book band.

Ella and the Imp
and
Dad Has a Nap

Written by
Robin Twiddy

Illustrated by
Maia Batumashvili

Can you say this sound and draw it with your finger?

Ella and the Imp

Illustrated by
Maia Batumashvili

Written by
Robin Twiddy

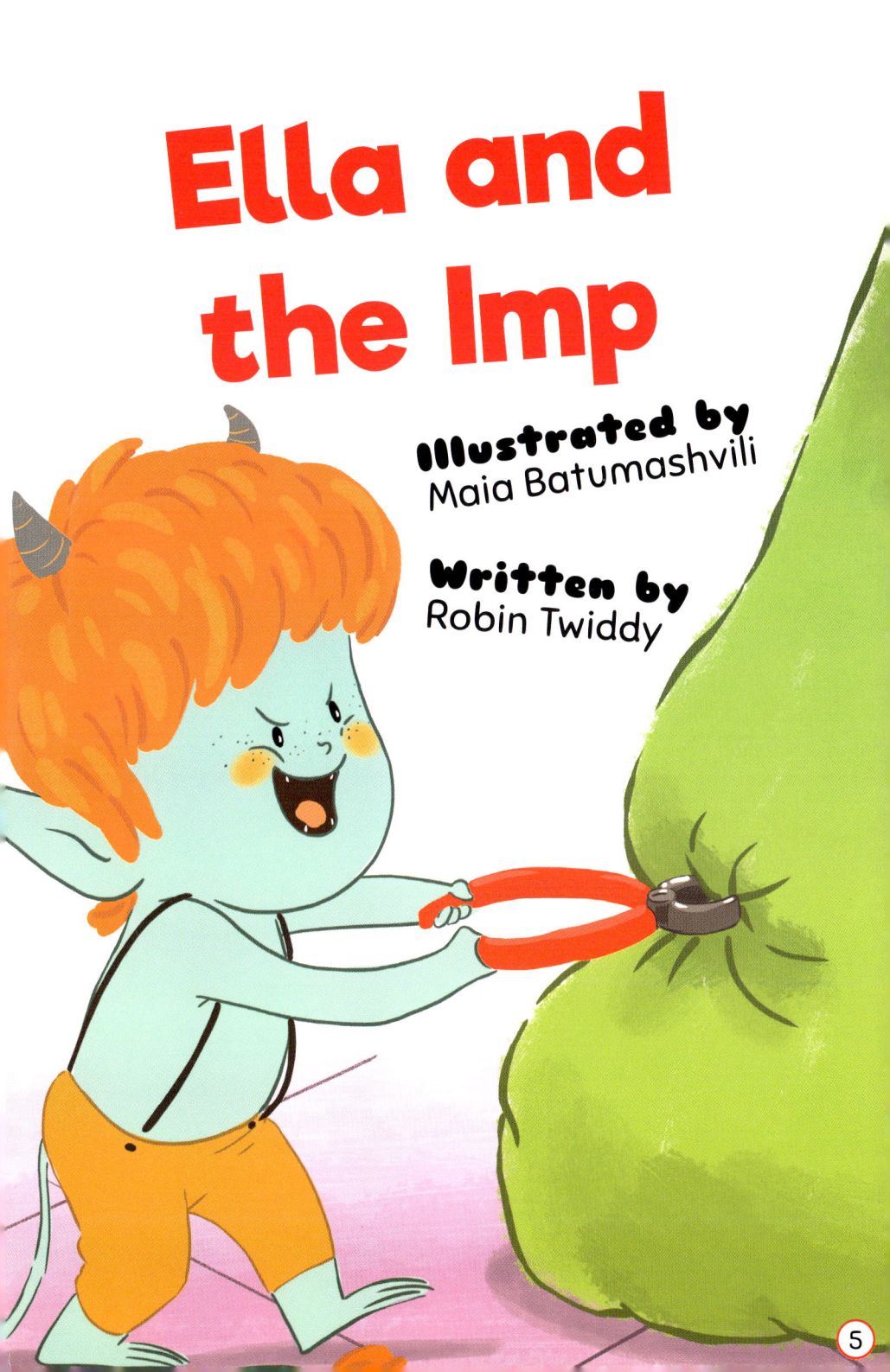

The imp has fun if it nips Mum.

The imp pulls the rug.

Mum has eggs. The imp pulls a leg.

The imp has fun if Mum is sad.

The imp puts a pin in. Mum jumps.

Mum is sad.

Ella is mad. She gets a mop.

The imp gets up to nip Mum's bum.

It is not Mum, it is a trap!

A bucket, a mop and a dress.

And Ella and a pot!

An imp in a pot.

Can you say this sound and draw it with your finger?

Dad Has a Nap

Written by
Robin Twiddy

Illustrated by
Maia Batumashvili

Dad had a nap.

Tom had a fun plan.

Tom put a pen on Dad.

Tim put a man on Dad.

Tim put a bot on Dad.

Tom put a bug on Dad.

Tim put a hot pot on Dad.

It is fun!

Tom put the dog on Dad.

The pen, man and bot fell off.

The pot, bug and dog fell off.

Dad fell off. Dad was mad!

BookLife PUBLISHING

©2020 **BookLife Publishing Ltd.**
King's Lynn, Norfolk PE30 4LS

ISBN 978-1-83927-278-3

All rights reserved. Printed in Malaysia.
A catalogue record for this book is available from the British Library.

Ella and the Imp & Dad Has a Nap
Written by Robin Twiddy
Illustrated by Maia Batumashvili

An Introduction to BookLife Readers...

Our Readers have been specifically created in line with the London Institute of Education's approach to book banding and are phonetically decodable and ordered to support each phase of the Letters and Sounds document.

Each book has been created to provide the best possible reading and learning experience. Our aim is to share our love of books with children, providing both emerging readers and prolific page-turners with beautiful books that are guaranteed to provoke interest and learning, regardless of ability.

BOOK BAND GRADED using the Institute of Education's approach to levelling.

PHONETICALLY DECODABLE supporting each phase of Letters and Sounds.

EXERCISES AND QUESTIONS to offer reinforcement and to ascertain comprehension.

BEAUTIFULLY ILLUSTRATED to inspire and provoke engagement, providing a variety of styles for the reader to enjoy whilst reading through the series.

AUTHOR INSIGHT:
ROBIN TWIDDY

Robin Twiddy is one of BookLife Publishing's most creative and prolific editorial talents, who imbues all his copy with a sense of adventure and energy. Robin's Cambridge-based first class honours degree in psychosocial studies offers a unique viewpoint on factual information and allows him to relay information in a manner that readers of any age are guaranteed to retain. He also holds a certificate in Teaching in the Lifelong Sector, and a post graduate certificate in Consumer Psychology.

A father of two, Robin has written over 70 titles for BookLife and specialises in conceptual, role-playing narratives which promote interaction with the reader and inspire even the most reluctant of readers to fully engage with his books.

PHASE 2 AND 3
2b

This book is a 'b' level and is a red level 2 book band.